We're All Going Places

CONTENTS

NATIONAL GEOGRAPHIC School Publishing

Hampton-Brown

al_
all

Words with al, all

Look at each picture. Read the words.

Example:

salt

wall

fall

bald

High Frequency Words
about
below
between
mountain
water
world

Key Words

Look at the picture.
Read the sentences.

The Tallest Falls

1. Look **between** the rocks at the tallest falls in the **world**.
2. The **water** drops **about** 2,650 feet.
3. It starts at the top of a **mountain**.
4. It crashes into the water far **below**.

Phonics Games
NGReach.com

The Tallest Falls

by Jean Paul Baptiste

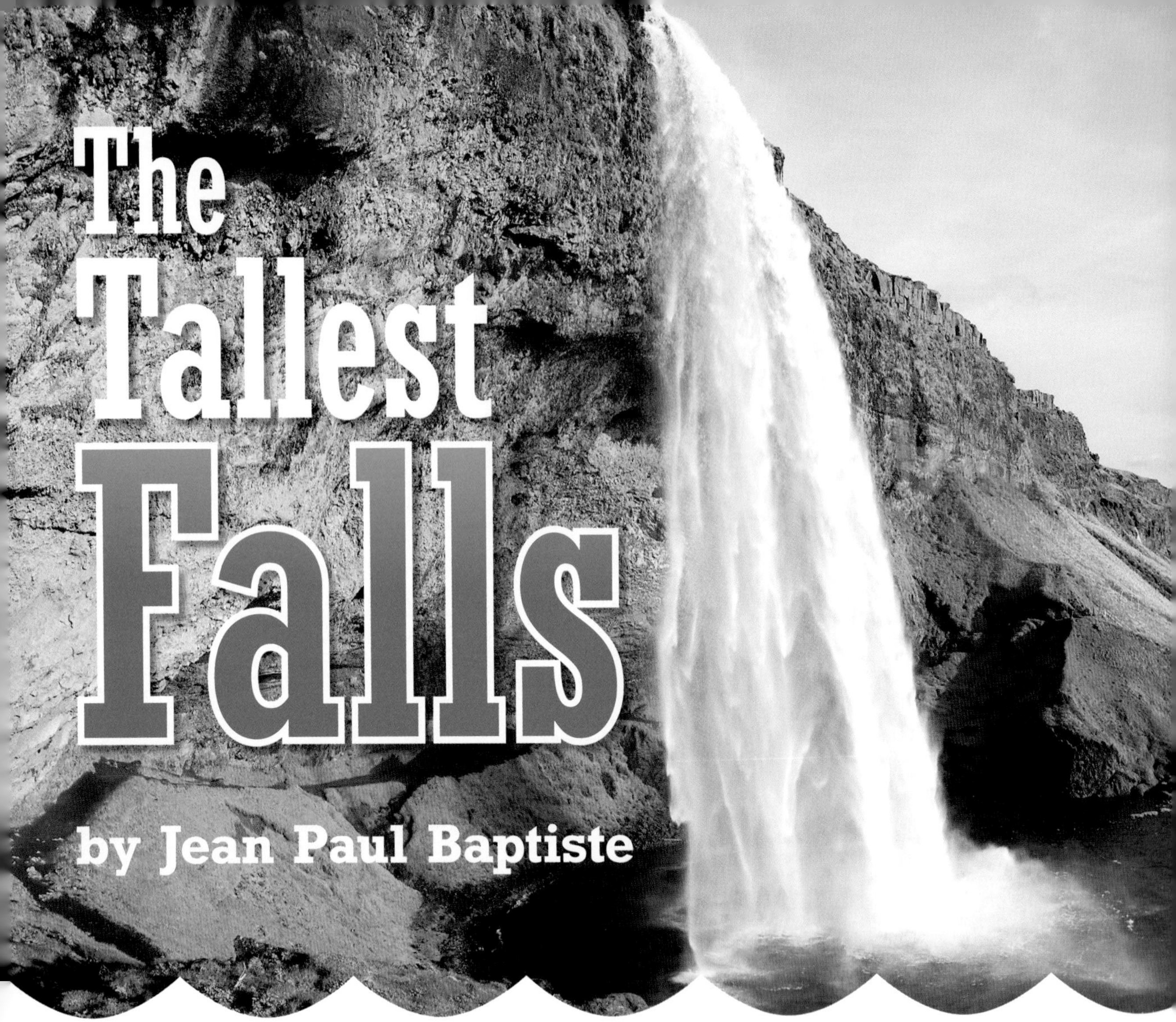

Rivers may start high up in mountains. What happens when water reaches the edge of a cliff? It falls. This makes a waterfall.

Falls can be small or tall, or any size in between. If the river is big, lots of water falls. If not, a thin stream falls.

Let's look at the tallest falls in the world. How tall are these falls? Think of buses, stacked end on end.

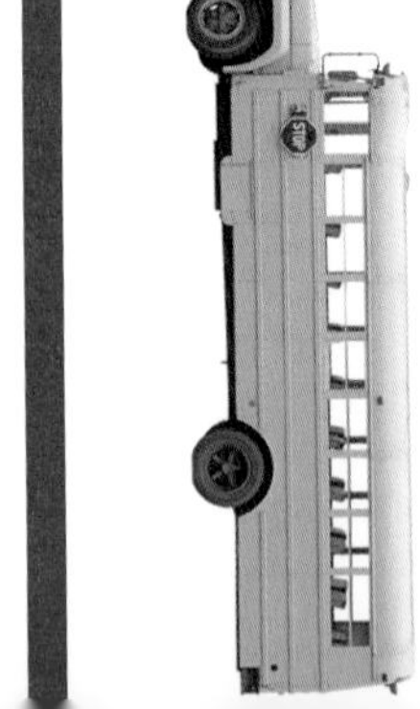

This world map shows where these tall falls are. Let's look at the tallest waterfall first.

These falls start far up on a mountain and drop way, way, WAY down. Wind turns water to mist and spray. Not much water reaches the bottom!

one part of Tugela Falls

This waterfall is smaller. It has five parts. Water falls into a pool below and keeps going. It does this five times.

Three Sisters Falls

This waterfall is called Three Sisters Falls. It has three parts. The third part can't be seen from the air. Tall trees grow on all sides.

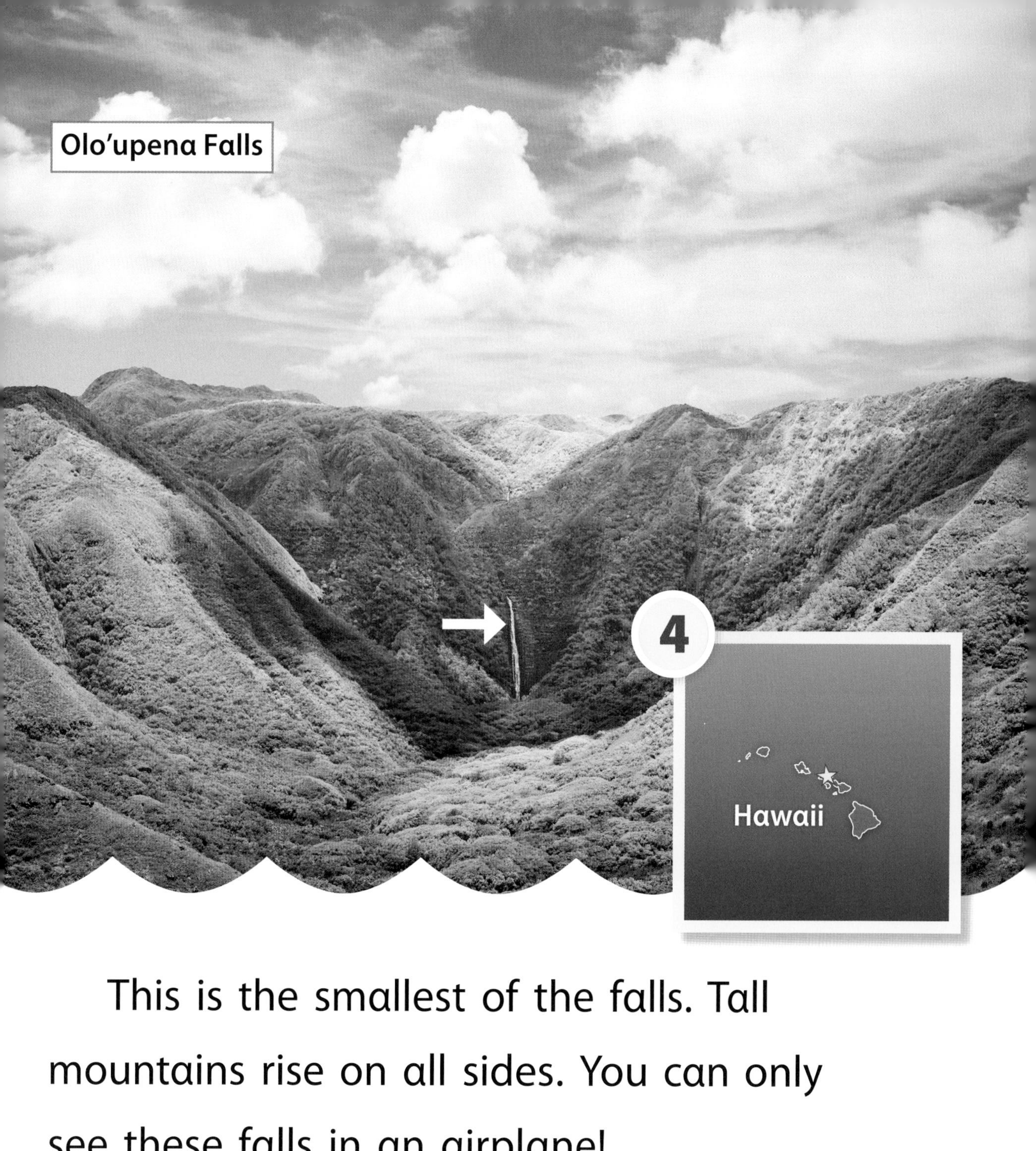

This is the smallest of the falls. Tall mountains rise on all sides. You can only see these falls in an airplane!

If a waterfall freezes, is it still a waterfall? Yes. Under the ice, some water still falls. Brrr! This is a tall waterfall. ❖

Words with al, all

Read these words.

falls	fast	mountain	call
tall	small	salt	lake

Find the words with **al** or **all**.
Use letters to build them.

c a l l

Talk Together

Choose words from the box above to tell your partner about each of these falls.

These falls are tall.

1.

2.

3.

Endings -es, -ed, -ing

Read each word pair. Sometimes the first word changes when you add the ending.

Example:

cry cri**es**

catch catch**es**

walk walk**ed**

hop hopp**ed**

slide slid**ing**

swing swing**ing**

High Frequency Words
about
below
between
mountain
water
world

Key Words

Read the sentences. Match each sentence to one of the pictures.

1. 

2. 

3. 

Plan a Fun Trip

1. You can hike up a **mountain** that is **about** a mile high.
2. You can go to Swim **World** and slide into the **water** **below**.
3. You can race in the water **between** the rocks.

Would you like water or a mountain best?

Phonics Games

NGReach.com

Good Map Skills

by Chris Medrick • illustrated by Alissia Girasole

The Starks were going on a road trip.

"Dad planned it," Mom said, smiling.

"I used these maps," Dad said, waving them.

Mel sighed.

"We're heading for Clear Lake State Park. It's in the mountains, about 40 miles away. Let's go!" Dad called. "Mom is driving!"

Mel hopped in the back seat.

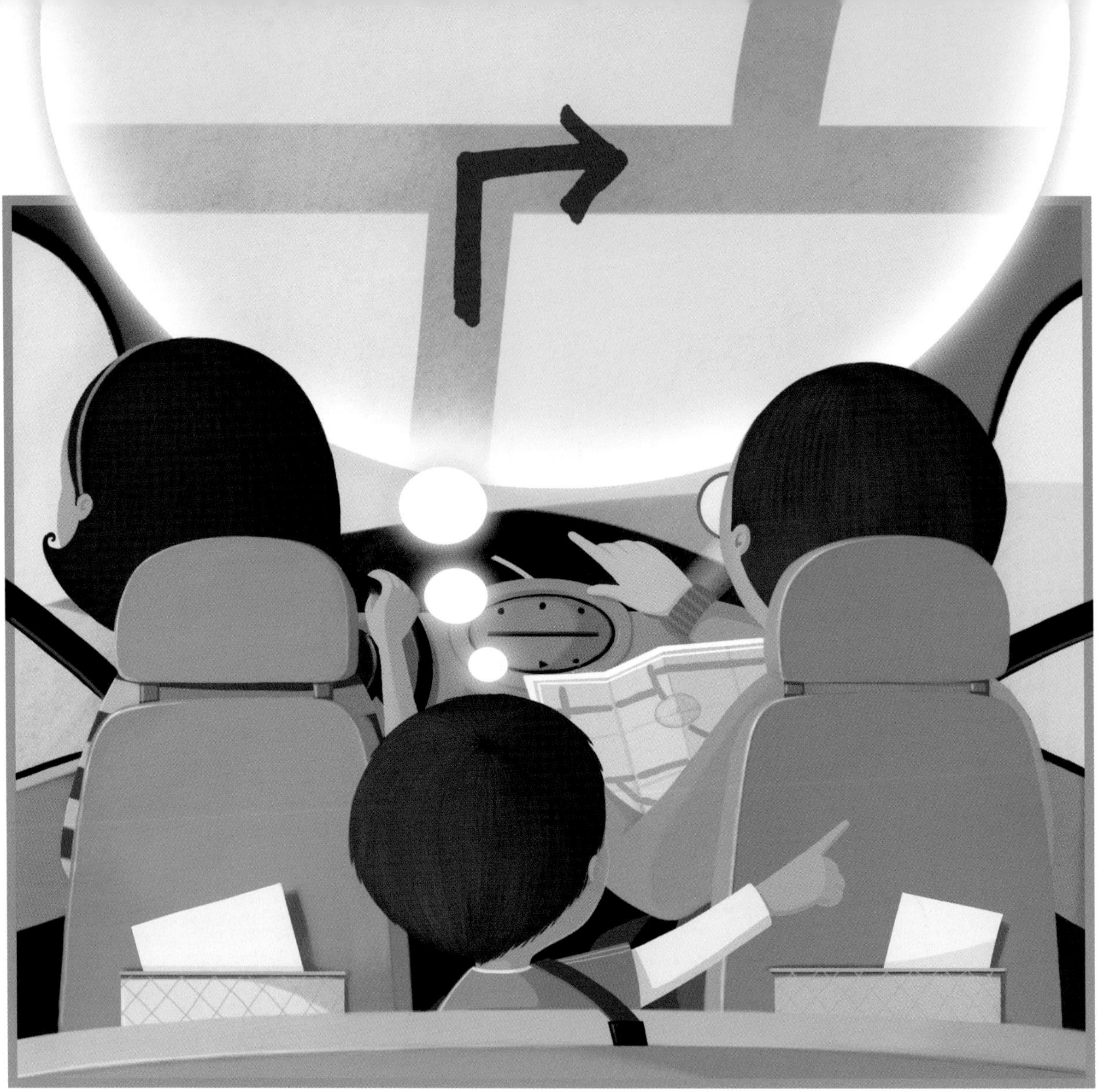

Dad looked at his maps. “Turn left,” he told Mom.

“No!” Mel cried. “Turn right!”

“Dad is looking at his maps,” Mom said. She turned left.

"Wood World? This isn't Clear Lake State Park," Dad said.

"Let's go back and turn right," said Mom.

Mel sighed.

"We're in the park. Turn right for Clear Lake," Dad told Mom.

"No!" Mel cried. "Turn left!"

"Dad is looking at his maps," Mom said. She turned right.

"Play World? This isn't Clear Lake," Dad said.

"Let's go back and turn left," said Mom.

Mel sighed.

"This isn't the right way," Dad said.

"Wait!" cried Mel. "I see water below. Keep going, Mom! Turn on the road between those two big rocks."

The Starks spread out their lunches on a picnic bench. Dad dragged two benches over. They all sat on them.

"So this is Clear Lake," Mom said. "It's nice!"

Dad grinned. “My maps are good,” he said. “But my map skills are not. Next time, Mel is helping me use these maps!”

Mel smiled. ❖

Endings -es, -ed, -ing

Read each word.

grinning	waved	flies	grinned
watches	munched	munching	waving

Point to the ending **-es**, **-ing**, or **-ed**. How does the word change when you add the ending? Use letters to build the words.

c r i e d

Talk Together

Choose words from the box. First tell your partner what each girl is doing. Then say what she did.

She is waving.
She waved.

Who Is Who?

Take turns with a partner. Pick a clue from the boxes. Read it. Put a marker in the box if you find it. Try to get three in a row.

Clues

Walt dropped a ball. **Find Walt.**	Claire is sitting on a wall between two lunchboxes. **Find Claire.**	Carmen is in the water, diving below the falls. **Find Carmen.**
Lin hiked up the mountain. **Find Lin.**	Mel and Jean are sitting on benches made of wood. **Find Mel.**	Juan walked in the woods to find the ball. **Find Juan.**
Mel and Jean are sitting on benches made of wood. **Find Jean.**	Claire is sitting on a wall between two lunchboxes. **Find a lunchbox.**	Juan walked in the woods to find the ball. **Find the woods.**

Acknowledgments
Grateful acknowledgment is given to the authors, artists, photographers, museums, publishers, and agents for permission to reprint copyrighted material. Every effort has been made to secure the appropriate permission. If any omissions have been made or if corrections are required, please contact the Publisher.

Photographic Credits
CVR (Cover) Corbis RF/Alamy Images. **2** (bl) Lisa Marzano/iStockphoto. (br) Alan D. Carey/PhotoDisc/Getty Images. (cl) DigitalStock/Corbis. (tl) Corbis. (tr) ilbusca/iStockphoto. **3** (b) Liz Garza Williams/Hampton-Brown/National Geographic School Publishing. (t) Edgar Quintero/National Geographic Image Collection. **4-5** (bg) Michael Utech/iStockphoto. **5** (b) Stacy Gold/National Geographic Image Collection. (c) Chris Leachman/iStockphoto. (t) Joshua Holder/iStockphoto. **6** (bg) John A. Rizzo Studio/PhotoDisc/Getty Images. (fg) Jon Patton/iStockphoto. (r-border) Jon Patton/iStockphoto. **8** (t) Edgar Quintero/National Geographic Image Collection. **8-9** (bg) Mezzografica/iStockphoto. **9** (t) Marek Patzer/AAI Fotostock/age fotostock. **10** (bg) Mezzografica/iStockphoto. (t) "Andes y Mares" & SEANTEC S.A.. **11** (t) Ed Freeman/Getty Images. **12** (bg) Mezzografica/iStockphoto. (fg) Arco Images GmbH/Alamy Images. **13** (bc) DigitalStock/Corbis. (bl) Edgar Quintero/National Geographic Image Collection. (br) blickwinkel/Alamy Images. (t) Liz Garza Williams/Hampton-Brown/National Geographic School Publishing. **14** (bl) Tim Pannell/Corbis/Jupiterimages. (br) mylife photos/Alamy Images. (cl) JJ pixs/Shutterstock. (cr) Michael Newman/PhotoEdit. (tl) Felix Mizioznikov/Shutterstock. (tr) Dallas John/iStockphoto. **15** (b) Liz Garza Williams/Hampton-Brown/National Geographic School Publishing. (tc) DigitalStock/Corbis. (tl) BostjanT/iStockphoto. (tr) Juriah Mosin/Shutterstock. **25** (t) Liz Garza Williams/Hampton-Brown/National Geographic School Publishing. **26** (tr) Sean MacD/Shutterstock.

Illustrator Credits
7-11 Mapping Specialists, Ltd.. **16-24** Alessia Girasole. **25-27** Natalia Vasquez

National Geographic School Publishing
Hampton-Brown
www.NGSP.com

Printed in the USA.
Quad Graphics, Leominster, MA

ISBN: 978-0-7362-8050-1

18 19
10 9 8 7 6

New High Frequency Words

- about
- below
- between
- mountain
- water
- world

Target Sound/Spellings

Words with al, all	Endings -es, -ed, -ing
Selection: **The Tallest Falls**	Selection: **Good Map Skills**
all	benches
called	called
falls	cried
small	dragged
smaller	driving
smallest	going
tall	grinned
tallest	heading
	helping
	hopped
	looked
	looking
	lunches
	planned
	sighed
	smiled
	smiling
	turned
	used
	waving